LAKE D
>> TRAIL RUNNING

20 OFF-ROAD ROUTES FOR
TRAIL & FELL RUNNERS

Published by Vertebrate Publishing, Sheffield
www.v-publishing.co.uk

LAKE DISTRICT
>> TRAIL RUNNING

20 OFF-ROAD ROUTES FOR
TRAIL & FELL RUNNERS

Helen Mort

Photography by Jan Bella

LAKE DISTRICT
>> TRAIL RUNNING
20 OFF-ROAD ROUTES FOR
TRAIL & FELL RUNNERS

VG Copyright © 2016 Helen Mort and Vertebrate Graphics Ltd.

VP First published in 2016 by Vertebrate Publishing.

Helen Mort has asserted her rights to be identified as the author of this work.

ISBN 978-1-910240-72-4

Front cover: Ben Wilkinson and Helen Mort in Langdale (route 6).
Back cover: Matthew Butler on the Troutbeck round (route 20).
All photography by Jan Bella.

 All maps reproduced by permission of Ordnancy Survey on behalf of The Controller of Her Majesty's Stationery Office. © Crown Copyright. 100025218.

VP Design by Jane Beagley, production by Nathan Ryder – www.v-publishing.co.uk

Printed in Europe by Pulsio.

MIX
Paper from
responsible sources
FSC® C128169
FSC
www.fsc.org

≫ CONTENTS

>> INTRODUCTION

When I moved to the Lake District for a year in 2010, I didn't really think of myself as a trail runner. I loved road running, but I was slightly daunted by some of the imposing fells that surrounded my home in Grasmere. But I bought a pair of trail shoes and started off on some of the routes that have made it into this book – Easedale, Loughrigg and Alcock Tarn. A few months later, I was racing for a local fell running club and running over the tops of mountains like Fairfield. I never looked back. And I never forgot the buzz of setting off from my door that first time, not quite knowing how the route would unfold.

I've tried to collect some of my favourite trail runs together in this guide. If you're already a seasoned fell runner, you probably have your own ideas about where to go in the Lakes. But if you're new to the area, or you're visiting on holiday and you want to get off-road and explore one of the most beautiful landscapes in the world, this book is for you. Some of these runs can be done before breakfast, while your family are still in bed, or they make a good evening run before a trip to one of the many pubs suggested. Others are more serious undertakings. Some of the shortest routes aren't always the easiest – they tackle steep terrain, making direct circuits of the fells. I've suggested a mixture of runs along the tops and easier, lakeside routes and, in some places, you can join a couple of runs together if you're looking for a longer day out.

Running in the Lake District presents its own particular challenges. Even some of the best paths can be awkward underfoot. The more popular destinations are often busy with tourists (and this book suggests doing those runs at quieter times). Finding parking spaces can be tricky. And that's before you consider the challenge of pitting yourself against gravity on the fellside, navigating bogs or finding your way in the infamous Lakeland weather. But every run offers a reward more than commensurate with the effort, and you'll see some of the best views the Lake District has to offer.

Most of these routes are clustered around the central Lakes area for ease of access, though some take you further afield. I've run them in all weathers and I've never failed to be surprised and delighted on the way. Trail running in the Lake District has given me some of the best days of my life and I hope it gives them to you too.

Happy running – enjoy the route, the view and the destination (especially if it's a fireside seat at the Kirkstile Inn).

Helen Mort

ACKNOWLEDGEMENTS

This book was written with the help of my dad, Andy Mort, who was too modest to want his name on the cover, but who spent months helping to plot, navigate and describe the routes as well as covering some of the miles with me. Thanks Dad, I still owe you at least eight pints in Tweedies.

Thanks also go to Ben Wilkinson, Phil Pickering, John Shedwick and most of all to Jan Bella and all the runners who modelled for photographs. Special thanks to all my friends in Grasmere and to Charlie and Bell, long-suffering trail-running whippets.

ABOUT THE ROUTES

The routes range in difficulty from relatively flat runs on lakeshore paths that should take less than an hour, to steep fell runs and upland epics that have the potential to take much longer. I have listed the runs within the book in order of increasing distance, but some of the shorter routes (such as Scales Tarn, page 21) involve sustained ascents. If you're unsure about your ability, aren't familiar with the area or come from a road-running background, start with some of the lower-level routes to gauge your level. Alcock Tarn (page 5) could be a good first test of your hill-running fitness.

MAPS

All the routes are carefully described and plotted on Ordnance Survey 1:25,000 mapping, but we strongly recommend that you carry the relevant full map (if for no other reason than it weighs less!) and a compass. Explorers OL4, OL5, OL6 and OL7 cover all the runs in this guide and are essential even if you are familiar with the area – you may need to cut short a run or take an alternative route. And of course, a map is no use without the navigational skills to use it.

DESCRIPTIONS, DISTANCES AND ASCENT

While every effort has been made to ensure accuracy within the maps and descriptions in this guide, we are unable to guarantee that every single detail is correct. Please exercise caution if a direction appears at odds with the route on the ground. If in doubt, a comparison between the directions, map and a bit of common sense should ensure you're on the right track.

Distances are in kilometres and height gain is in metres. Both were measured using GPS devices on the runs, but we cannot promise that they are 100% accurate, so please treat stated distances as a guideline only. Our estimated times are a combination of optimism, generosity, challenge and fiction; just allow plenty of time and try to run an even pace.

TERRAIN

I have attempted to describe the terrain on each route, but most Lake District runs involve a bit of everything. Route conditions can be dramatically influenced by the weather. Streams become swollen, rocks slippery and moorland boggy. Visibility can affect your ability to navigate and there are some routes in this guide – Fairfield Horseshoe, Troutbeck and Haweswater in particular – that shouldn't be attempted in bad weather unless you are a very experienced trail runner. Where a route involves fording a stream, it may not be easy to cross after heavy rainfall. Take account of the conditions – if in doubt, there are routes in this book like the Rydal and Coffin Path route or Buttermere that can be run in most weathers.

RECOMMENDED EQUIPMENT

Recommended kit varies depending on the time of year and the difficulty and nature of the route. While many runners like the freedom of a 'fast and light' approach, longer and more remote runs are best undertaken with a little more kit.

» **Bag**: there are plenty of lightweight rucksacks and bumbags on the market.
  Find one that's comfy and doesn't move around on rough ground.
» **Waterproofs/windproofs**: jacket and trousers. We'd strongly recommend fully
  waterproof with taped seams; this is the Lake District.
» **Hat and gloves**: keep your extremities warm and the rest will follow.
  It's no fun fumbling with shoelaces with frozen fingers.
» **Map and compass**: and know how to use them! The relevant maps are
  listed on page viii.
» **Whistle**: Six short blasts in quick succession means 'help!'
» **Space blanket and small first aid kit**: weighs nothing, takes up hardly any room
  and could save your life.
» **Food and water**: enough for your expected duration of the run
  and some emergency rations.
» **Headtorch**: if you're heading out late, a headtorch should be high
  on your list of essentials.

FOOTWEAR

We'd recommend at least 'trail' shoes for all these routes, with fell shoes being desirable on the harder routes. Trail shoes offer more grip and greater stability than road shoes, while the deep lugs on the soles of fell shoes will come in handy on boggy or wet ground.

CLOTHING

Dress appropriately for the season. Shorts and a vest work well on hot summer days, but thermals, windproofs and gloves are better on winter runs. Please note that exposure on higher ground is a very real risk for the tired, lost or slowing runner – better to carry a small bag with full waterproofs and gloves/hat, than be flapping around on the top of Fairfield trying to get a signal and call out mountain rescue.

FUEL AND HYDRATION

Hot days can be deadly for the trail runner. We don't recommend drinking from any streams in the Lake District, so carry sufficient water (either in bottles or a hydration pack) for your run. Likewise, a banana or two and an 'emergency' gel can come in handy, especially on long days out.

SAFETY

Ideally, run in pairs, tell someone where you are going and carry a phone – but note that finding good reception is difficult in many parts of the Lake District. Should you find yourself out of reception, be grateful to be temporarily free of the phone's tyranny.

MOUNTAIN RESCUE AND MOUNTAIN RESCUE BY SMS TEXT

In case of an accident or similar requiring mountain rescue assistance, dial **999** and ask for **POLICE – MOUNTAIN RESCUE**. Be prepared to give a 6-figure grid reference of your position in the case of an upland location.

Another option in the UK is contacting the emergency services by SMS text – useful if you have a low battery or intermittent signal. You need to register first – text 'register' to 999 and then follow the instructions in the reply. **www.emergencysms.org.uk**

Do it now – it could save a life!

Pete Bland Sports opened in 1981 and is now one of the leading running specialists in the UK. Pete and Anne Bland were the brains and motivation behind the dream and are largely responsible for its continuing success. Pete and Anne's son Matthew has handled the day to day running of the business for the last 20 years.

We feel we offer the most comprehensive range of fell, trail and road shoes for both men and women, complemented by a selection of racing shoes and track spikes. Whatever the running season we have the clothing to match. Come snow, wind, sun or rain (and it does up here!) Pete Bland Sports can keep you comfortable while running. Heart rate, speed distance monitors, watches and running accessories only add to what is the true meaning of a running retailer.

COUNTRYSIDE CODE

BE SAFE – PLAN AHEAD

Even when going out locally, it's best to get the latest information about where and when you can go; for example, your rights to go on to some areas of open land may be restricted while work is carried out, for safety reasons or during breeding seasons. Follow advice and local signs, and be prepared for the unexpected.

» Refer to up-to-date maps or guidebooks.
» You're responsible for your own safety and for others in your care, so be prepared for changes in weather and other events.
» There are many organisations offering specific advice on equipment and safety, or contact visitor information centres and libraries for a list of outdoor recreation groups.
» Check weather forecasts before you leave, and don't be afraid to turn back.
» Part of the appeal of the countryside is that you can get away from it all. You may not see anyone for hours and there are many places without clear mobile phone signals, so let someone else know where you're going and when you expect to return.

LEAVE GATES AND PROPERTY AS YOU FIND THEM

Please respect the working life of the countryside, as our actions can affect people's livelihoods, our heritage, and the safety and welfare of animals and ourselves.

» A farmer will normally leave a gate closed to keep livestock in, but may sometimes leave it open so they can reach food and water. Leave gates as you find them or follow instructions on signs; if walking in a group, make sure the last person knows how to leave the gates.
» In fields where crops are growing, follow the paths wherever possible.
» Use gates and stiles wherever possible – climbing over walls, hedges and fences can damage them and increase the risk of farm animals escaping.
» Our heritage belongs to all of us – be careful not to disturb ruins and historic sites.
» Leave machinery and livestock alone – don't interfere with animals even if you think they're in distress. Try to alert the farmer instead.

PROTECT PLANTS AND ANIMALS, AND TAKE YOUR LITTER HOME

We have a responsibility to protect our countryside now and for future generations, so make sure you don't harm animals, birds, plants or trees.

» Litter and leftover food doesn't just spoil the beauty of the countryside, it can be dangerous to wildlife and farm animals and can spread disease – so take your litter home with you. Dropping litter and dumping rubbish are criminal offences.

» Discover the beauty of the natural environment and take special care not to damage, destroy or remove features such as rocks, plants and trees. They provide homes and food for wildlife, and add to everybody's enjoyment of the countryside.

» Wild animals and farm animals can behave unpredictably if you get too close, especially if they're with their young – so give them plenty of space.

» Fires can be as devastating to wildlife and habitats as they are to people and property – so be careful not to drop a match or smouldering cigarette at any time of the year. Sometimes, controlled fires are used to manage vegetation, particularly on heaths and moors between October and early April, so please check that a fire is not supervised before calling 999.

KEEP DOGS UNDER CLOSE CONTROL

The countryside is a great place to exercise dogs, but it is owners' duty to make sure their dog is not a danger or nuisance to farm animals, wildlife or other people.

» By law, you must control your dog so that it does not disturb or scare farm animals or wildlife. You must keep your dog on a short lead on most areas of open country and common land between 1 March and 31 July, and at all times near farm animals.

» You do not have to put your dog on a lead on public paths as long as it is under close control. But as a general rule, keep your dog on a lead if you cannot rely on its obedience. By law, farmers are entitled to destroy a dog that injures or worries their animals.

» If a farm animal chases you and your dog, it is safer to let your dog off the lead – don't risk getting hurt by trying to protect it.

» Take particular care that your dog doesn't scare sheep and lambs or wander where it might disturb birds that nest on the ground and other wildlife – eggs and young will soon die without protection from their parents.

» Everyone knows how unpleasant dog mess is and it can cause infections – so always clean up after your dog and get rid of the mess responsibly. Also make sure your dog is wormed regularly.

CONSIDER OTHER PEOPLE

Showing consideration and respect for other people makes the countryside a pleasant environment for everyone – at home, at work and at leisure.

» Busy traffic on small country roads can be unpleasant and dangerous to local people, visitors and wildlife – so slow down and, where possible, leave your vehicle at home, consider sharing lifts and use alternatives such as public transport or cycling. For public transport information, phone Traveline on 0871 200 2233.

» Respect the needs of local people – for example, don't block gateways, driveways or other entry points with your vehicle.

» By law, cyclists must give way to walkers and horse riders on bridleways.

» Keep out of the way when farm animals are being gathered or moved and follow directions from the farmer.

» Support the rural economy – for example, buy your supplies from local shops.

CONTAINS ORDNANCE SURVEY DATA © CROWN COPYRIGHT AND DATABASE RIGHT.

LAKE DISTRICT TRAIL RUNNING
AREA
MAP

THE
TRAILS

Trail running in the Lake District can offer you some of the most sublime views and experiences you can have as a runner, but other times it can be wet, boggy, cold and lonely. Some days you'll be flying with a vista of the fells, others you'll be running misty miles alone, getting lost, doubling back, or plodding through puddles, wishing you'd not stayed in Tweedies Bar quite so long the night before. But even on a bad day, I've never been on a run in the Lake District I've regretted, even for a second. Through this book, I've tried to share some of my favourites with you, from well-worn trails to more ambitious circuits of the hills. I've emphasised shorter, accessible routes that you can work into your day, but many of the short runs come with a testing climb. So plan your routes carefully, take plenty of supplies, get your trail shoes on and head for the hills!

THE SHORT-BUT-STEEP PATH TO ALCOCK TARN

01 ›› ALCOCK TARN

5.1km

INTRODUCTION

Alcock Tarn overlooks Grasmere vale and is used for the annual Grasmere Senior Guides fell race which goes up to Butter Crag, though the race route takes a steeper path up the hillside than the one described here (you may find this hard to believe as you near the top!). Our route takes us past Greenhead Gill, which was once an Elizabethan lead mine, though there's now little to see on the ground and it's hard to imagine this quiet, placid valley as industrial.

THE ROUTE

This is the shortest route in the book but not necessarily the easiest. We run steeply up the hillside and descend just as steeply on the other side, after a brief, flatter section passing the tarn. A good test of fitness before attempting something like Blencathra or Fairfield Horseshoe, and excellent training for some of the bigger hills. After the abrupt downhill, we run back through flat fields to the village.

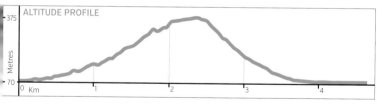

›› ALCOCK TARN

DISTANCE: 5.1KM ›› *ASCENT:* 305M ›› *MAX ALTITUDE:* 375M ›› *TYPICAL TIME:* 0:45 HRS ›› *TERRAIN:* MOSTLY ROUGH PATHS, SOME TARMAC ›› *NAVIGATION:* STRAIGHTFORWARD ›› *START/FINISH:* STOCK LANE CAR PARK ›› *GRID REF:* NY 339072 ›› *SATNAV:* LA22 9SJ ›› *OS MAP:* OL7 THE ENGLISH LAKES SOUTH-EASTERN AREA ›› *REFRESHMENTS:* TWEEDIES BAR, GRASMERE TEL: 01539 435 300

DIRECTIONS >> ALCOCK TARN

S Start from Stock Lane car park in Grasmere and head out of the village, crossing the A591 towards The Wordsworth Trust and Dove Cottage. Passing the Cottage on your left, climb steeply up the hill until you reach a turn-off. **Turn left** (signposted *No through road*). 180m after the junction **turn left** along a rough track signposted *Alcock Tarn*.

2 This track takes you all the way to the top of Alcock Tarn, passing through mixed beech woods and skirting a small pond before curving up to the fellside. The route is well signposted at each gate you pass through and is mostly steep, with a few flatter sections for respite.

3 Near the top, contour round beneath Grey Crag and climb the grassy shoulder until you can see the tarn. Don't forget to turn back to take in the wonderful views of Grasmere vale and Windermere! Traverse left by the tarn, with Great Rigg ahead, and the path begins to descend.

4 The path zigzags steeply down above the forestry wall and is rocky underfoot in places. When you reach Greenhead Gill, follow it to the wooden footbridge where you cross. A surfaced track takes you to The Swan Inn and the A591.

5 Cross the road and **turn left** to run alongside it, before taking the **second** of two public footpaths on your **right**, directing you across the fields back to Stock Lane car park. You could detour to the village and to Tweedies Bar on your way back too if the climb has left you thirsty.

JENNY WONG ON THE CLIMB TO BARROW FROM BRAITHWAITE

INTRODUCTION

Barrow is a small but very striking fell enclosed by the ridges of Coledale. Its distinctive shape and the grassy path zigzagging up it catch your eye from the A66. Barrow and its neighbour Outerside remain relatively unvisited, so this steady 5k offers peace and quiet as well as views of Blencathra, Keswick and Derwentwater.

THE ROUTE

There is no official car park in Braithwaite but there are usually plenty of corners to park in. Leaving the village towards the Newlands Valley, the path up Barrow is grassy and wide. The return route is just as inviting and easy underfoot – about as good as you'll get on Lake District trails. There's the option of extending this run from Barrow Door over to Outerside if you like, making a 7km circuit returning via Coledale Beck.

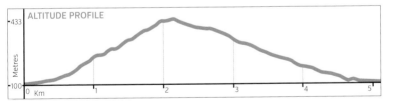

ALTITUDE PROFILE

» BARROW

DISTANCE: 5.2KM » **ASCENT:** 352M » **MAX ALTITUDE:** 433M » **TYPICAL TIME:** 0:45 HRS » **TERRAIN:** GRASS, STONY PATHS » **NAVIGATION:** STRAIGHTFORWARD » **START/FINISH:** BRAITHWAITE » **GRID REF:** NY 230236 **SATNAV:** CA12 5SY » **OS MAP:** EXPLORER OL4 THE ENGLISH LAKES NORTH-WESTERN AREA **REFRESHMENTS:** COLEDALE INN, BRAITHWAITE TEL: 01768 778 272

DIRECTIONS >> BARROW

S Park in Braithwaite and follow road signs towards the Newlands Valley. As you start to leave the village, **turn right** on to a track with a cattle grid and a public footpath sign leading up to Braithwaite Lodge. Follow this to the lodge, where the path onwards is well signed.

2 At the gate, go straight on – signposted *Newlands* – and **bear left** up the fell. When you reach a fingerpost, **bear right** (signposted *Barrow*).

3 A wide grassy track climbs up and over Barrow. After the first high point, you descend to a cairn and then climb again. After the second stretch of descent, you reach a junction of paths at Barrow Door.

4 Take the path on the **right**, back down towards Braithwaite. The narrow, pleasant path you run down eventually becomes more of a surfaced track. Pass through a gate to join a small road. Either follow this back to Braithwaite or turn right at a public footpath sign to return to Braithwaite Lodge and retrace your steps from there.

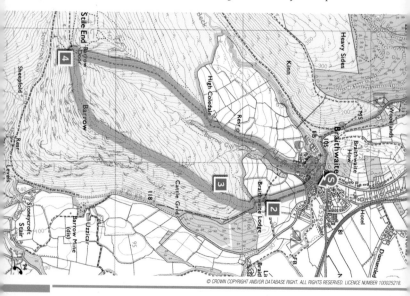

EASY, STONY PATHS ON BARROW

ANA BARBE CATCHES SUNSET OVER TORVER COMMON

03 » TORVER COMMON & CONISTON SHORE

5.6km

INTRODUCTION

A short drive from Coniston, Torver stands on the old packhorse route to the Duddon Valley and used to boast a railway line to transport slate. This run starts on Torver Common and takes in the shore of Coniston Water, the third largest lake in the Lake District. Arthur Ransome's novel *Swallows and Amazons* is set around a fictional lake which is believed to be a combination of Windermere and Coniston, and, looking out to the fells, you can see how the setting has inspired many a work of art.

THE ROUTE

Though short, this is a varied, scenic run. The knolls you climb on the way out give views of the Coniston fells, Red Screes and Fairfield. The path by the lake shore is shaded and pleasant, though you have to negotiate rocks and tree roots. Even the short section of road at the end offers an excellent vista!

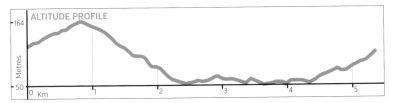

» TORVER COMMON & CONISTON SHORE

DISTANCE: 5.6KM » *ASCENT:* 102M » *MAX ALTITUDE:* 164M » *TYPICAL TIME:* 0:40 HRS » *TERRAIN:* GRASS, NARROW WOODLAND PATHS, SHORT ROAD SECTION » *NAVIGATION:* INITIALLY A BIT FIDDLY, EASY ONCE YOU REACH THE LAKESIDE » *START/FINISH:* LAKELAND LAND ROVER GARAGE » *GRID REF:* SD 287932
SATNAV: LA21 8BJ » *OS MAP:* EXPLORER OL6 THE ENGLISH LAKES SOUTH-WESTERN AREA
REFRESHMENTS: RETURN TO CONISTON FOR A CHOICE OF PUBS AND CAFES

DIRECTIONS ≫ TORVER COMMON & CONISTON SHORE

S   Park above the A5084 opposite the Lakeland Land Rover garage and take the track above the parking space to a kissing gate which leads out on to the hilly common.

2   Take the grassy path **left**, passing Kelly Hall Tarn and Long Moss Tarn. The path travels over a series of knolls. As a rule, keep the wall on your left as a guide over the hillside.

3   As the path descends, cross a little stream and contour the hillside below a stone wall. This path soon bears left and takes you into woodland. Follow the obvious tracks through the woods all the way to the shore of Coniston Water.

4   At the lake, **turn right** and run along the lakeside path close to the water. Follow this all the way to Sunny Bank jetty, where the path climbs away from the lake to the right, following a wall.

5   Where this path forks, take the higher path on the **right** which skirts round Delicars enclosure and comes out at the road. **Turn right**. A short section of road running returns you to the car park.

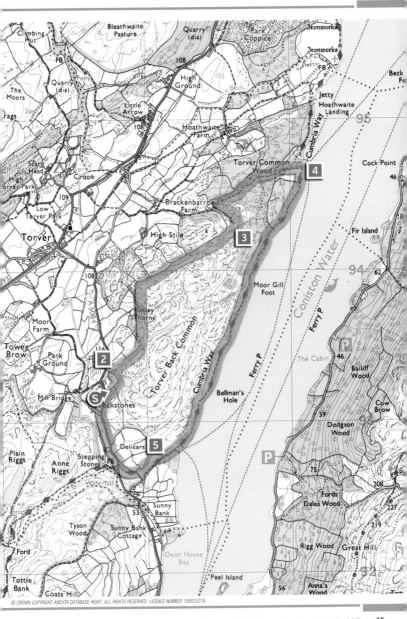

KARL MASON ON THE EDGE OF SCOUT SCAR

INTRODUCTION

Scout Scar is a long limestone escarpment not far from Kendal, and this run along the edge of it and back across the hillside is a gentle excursion which could easily be done before breakfast if in the South Lakes. The route offers views of the Lakeland fells and also the Howgills to the east.

THE ROUTE

This is one of the easiest routes in the book – excellent underfoot all the way and straightforward to navigate. The climbs are gentle, but the views are rewarding all the same – we retrace our steps at the end of the run but get an altogether different view back towards Kendal.

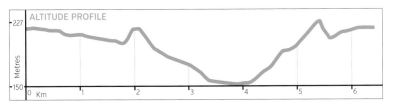

ALTITUDE PROFILE

» **SCOUT SCAR**

DISTANCE: 6.5KM » *ASCENT:* 112M » *MAX ALTITUDE:* 227M » *TYPICAL TIME:* 0:45 HRS » *TERRAIN:* MOSTLY GRASSY PATHS » *NAVIGATION:* EASY » *START/FINISH:* SCOUT SCAR CAR PARK » *GRID REF:* SD 488924 *SATNAV:* LA8 8HA [NEAREST] » *OS MAP:* EXPLORER OL7 THE ENGLISH LAKES SOUTH-EASTERN AREA *REFRESHMENTS:* CHOICE OF PUBS AND CAFES IN KENDAL

DIRECTIONS >> SCOUT SCAR

S Park at the Scout Scar car park (free parking) and cross the road, taking the path through the gate opposite the car park. The path climbs to join the edge above the Scar. Follow this south for just over a mile, staying close to the edge.

2 At a large cairn/pile of stones, **turn left** and follow the path all the way to Brigsteer Road, passing through two kissing gates along the way.

3 Pass through a squeezer stile in the wall to join the road. **Turn left**. Just after the sign for Kendal, **turn left** over a wall stile by gates and follow a public footpath signed to *Scout Scar*, heading towards Bradley Field farm.

4 This grassy path skirts to the left of the farm, passing through a gate and staying close to the wall. Follow this all the way back to the path along the edge of Scout Scar you ran along at the beginning of your run. **Turn right** and retrace your steps back to the car park.

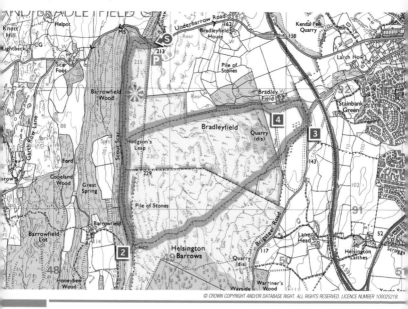

ONE MAN AND HIS DOG: MATT LE VOI AT SCALES TARN

05 » SCALES TARN

7.2km

INTRODUCTION

An exciting, tough fell run which contours round Scales Tarn and skirts Blencathra, providing dramatic views up to Sharp Edge. This is only a short route, but it makes up for it in quality (and gradient). Blencathra is one of the most northerly of the Lake District fells and is also known as 'Saddleback' because of its distinctive shape when seen from the east.

THE ROUTE

Narrow paths head up Scales Fell from the village of Scales, then climb to a shoulder. There's an enjoyable, flatter section with exhilarating views as you run to Scales Tarn, then a tough climb towards the summit of Blencathra. Here, you have the choice of veering right to reach the summit or turning left and taking the good path back down the fell until it rejoins your original path up from Scales.

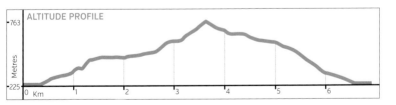

ALTITUDE PROFILE

» SCALES TARN

DISTANCE: 7.2KM » *ASCENT:* 542M » *MAX ALTITUDE:* 763M » *TYPICAL TIME:* 1 HR » *TERRAIN:* MOSTLY ROUGH PATHS, SOME TARMAC » *NAVIGATION:* MODERATE – LOTS OF ALTERNATIVE PATHS SHORTLY AFTER LEAVING SCALES WHICH MAY CAUSE CONFUSION » *START/FINISH:* SCALES VILLAGE » *GRID REF:* NY 343269 » *SATNAV:* CA12 4SY » *OS MAP:* EXPLORER OL5 THE ENGLISH LAKES NORTH-EASTERN AREA *REFRESHMENTS:* WHITE HORSE INN, SCALES TEL: 01768 779 883

DIRECTIONS >> SCALES TARN

S   Park in the village of Scales. To join the path for this route, run alongside the A66 for a short stretch, **turning right** just before the last house at a public footpath sign.

2   Take the **right fork** through the gate and follow the higher narrow track up the hillside rather than the path that sticks close to the wall. Ignore the grassy tracks you pass to your left.

3   When you reach a crossroads in the path, **bear right** (the path on the left will be your descent) and climb steeply up the shoulder.

4   At the top you reach a crossroads, marked by a stone. **Go straight ahead** along the path, ignoring those to the left and right. You'll see Sharp Edge ahead of you and enjoy a section of flat running with striking views.

5   Where you cross Scales Beck, climb a series of stone steps. Just before the tarn, **take the left fork** – the right leads up to Sharp Edge, which isn't running terrain! At the edge of the tarn, **bear left** again and climb the fellside.

6   At the top, **bear left** (unless you'd like to detour to the top of Blencathra, just off to your right). Join an obvious path which leads down the ridge and take the **right-hand fork** where it divides.

7   After a steep descent, you arrive back at the crossroads you were at earlier. Retrace the path back down to the A66, then the road to Scales.

HIGH ON THE BLENCATHRA ROUTE, JUST BEFORE THE FINAL CLIMB

EMMA RYAN STRIDING OUT ALONG THE SHORE AT BUTTERMERE ≫ ROUTE 7

BEN WILKINSON AND HELEN MORT IN LANGDALE

06 >> LANGDALE LOOP

7.3km

INTRODUCTION

Langdale has a wonderful feeling of remoteness, even though it is popular with cyclists, walkers, campers and drinkers visiting the Old Dungeon Ghyll. This run passes under the Langdale Pikes, where you can glimpse a host of classic climbing routes. It isn't a challenging route, but crossing the ford adds an element of adventure.

THE ROUTE

A rough track takes you out past the pubs of Langdale and the return journey is via a series of smoother tracks, brief stretches of road and grassy paths. Getting across the river may be a challenge. At the time of writing, a bridge seemed to be under construction and was not yet finished. Even in skeletal form, it offered an airy traverse. Best avoid this route in the depths of winter or after a period of heavy rainfall when the river may be particularly high.

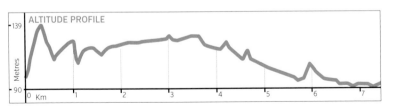

ALTITUDE PROFILE

>> **LANGDALE LOOP**

DISTANCE: 7.3KM >> *ASCENT:* 72M >> *MAX ALTITUDE:* 139M >> *TYPICAL TIME:* 0:45 HRS >> *TERRAIN:* MOSTLY ROUGH, STONY PATHS. AWKWARD RIVER CROSSING >> *NAVIGATION:* MODERATE >> *START/FINISH:* NEW DUNGEON GHYLL >> *GRID REF:* NY 295064 >> *SATNAV:* LA22 9JX >> *OS MAP:* EXPLORER OL7 THE ENGLISH LAKES SOUTH-EASTERN AREA >> *REFRESHMENTS:* NEW DUNGEON GHYLL TEL: 01539 437 213

DIRECTIONS >> LANGDALE LOOP

S Start from the New Dungeon Ghyll (parking at the pub or at Sticklebarn) and take the gate just behind the pub.

2 Continue through a field, then a gap in a stone wall just beyond and **turn left** at a junction along the rough path above the wall. This uneven track (with walls to either side) takes you out beneath the Langdale Pikes, passing the Old Dungeon Ghyll on the way.

3 When the fields to your left end and you reach the last of the wall, **turn immediately left** and descend to the river. You should be able to cross here via a bridge (of sorts) or perhaps a ford, depending on the water level. (If you cannot cross here, you can continue up to a mile up the dale where crossing might be easier.) **Turn left** on the other side to join a rough footpath.

4 Follow the path to Stool End farm where signs direct you through to a road beyond and then to the public road. **Turn right** here and cross the bridge, then **turn left** into Great Langdale campsite.

5 At the far right corner of the campsite, go through a gate, cross a footbridge and climb through a band of trees to reach a gate into a field. Midway through this field **turn left** to join a faint footpath across the slope. Follow this to Side House and then the path cuts left to a driveway – take this to return towards the New Dungeon Ghyll.

LANGDALE

EASY UNDERFOOT AT BUTTERMERE

INTRODUCTION

Buttermere's name means 'the lake by the dairy pastures' and you can enjoy a steady, flat trail run around it, flanked by the High Stile range, Fleetwith Pike and Haystacks. There's a small surprise on the way back for which you may want to bring a headtorch! All will be revealed as you run along the north-eastern shore.

THE ROUTE

This run starts from the centre of Buttermere (with its choice of good pubs) and starts out along the south-western shore of the lake. There's virtually no ascent on this run and the paths are mostly easy – on a dry day, your main problem will be dodging walkers. Again, this run might be best enjoyed early in the morning before the paths become popular.

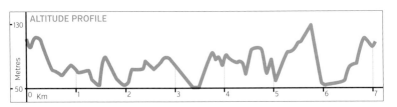

ALTITUDE PROFILE

» **BUTTERMERE**

DISTANCE: 7.5KM » *ASCENT:* 30M » *MAX ALTITUDE:* 130M » *TYPICAL TIME:* 0:40 HRS » *TERRAIN:* GOOD PATHS, ROCKY AT TIMES » *NAVIGATION:* VERY EASY » *START/FINISH:* BUTTERMERE VILLAGE *GRID REF:* NY 172169 » *SATNAV:* CA13 9XA » *OS MAP:* EXPLORER OL4 THE ENGLISH LAKES NORTH-WESTERN AREA » *REFRESHMENTS:* THE FISH INN TEL: 01768 770 253

DIRECTIONS ≫ BUTTERMERE

S   Start from the centre of Buttermere and take the fenced path that runs alongside the Fish Inn hotel. This path turns left, goes through a gate and leads you towards Buttermere lake. **Turn right** and follow the path along the field edge to the bridge. Cross and **bear left** to another bridge and gate. Go through this and **bear left** to follow the lake shore.

2   You now follow the shore for a few kilometres. Occasionally there's a choice of paths, both leading to the same place – the route closest to the lake is usually the most scenic.

3   At the end of the lake, **turn left** through the gate, cross Peggy's Bridge, and run along the lane up to Gatesgarth Farm. **Keep left** through the yard, separated by a fence, up to the road. **Turn left** here and follow the road up a slight rise until you see a small path off left which leads back down to the shore – take this.

4   Following the lake shore back to Buttermere, you'll have the surreal experience of passing through a dark tunnel hewn from rock. This is the point where you might want to use your headtorch – briefly – if you have brought one!

5   Approaching the end of the lake, go through the gate and then **bear left** and go through another gate to continue round the shoreline back to the National Trust's field. **Turn right**, go through the gate and back into the lane to Buttermere village.

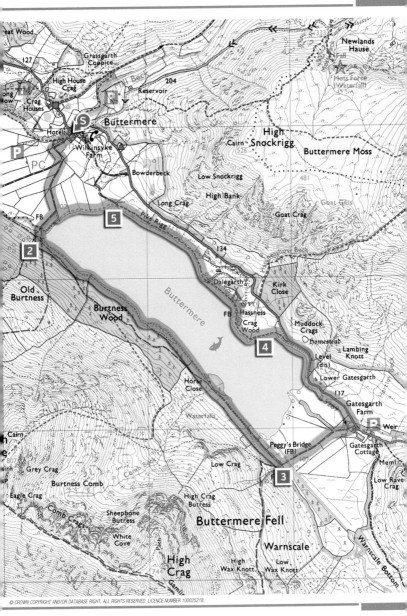

CROSSING THE TOP OF EASEDALE TARN BEFORE THE DESCENT TO GRASMERE

08 >> EASEDALE TARN

8km

INTRODUCTION

Proof that you don't have to gain a summit to get fantastic Lakeland views, this is a moderate climb up to a placid tarn, with views of waterfalls, fells and meandering Herdwick sheep to amuse you on the way. Dorothy Wordsworth called Easedale 'the black quarter', because the dark rocks can take on a slightly menacing appearance in bad weather, but poet Thomas De Quincey declared it 'a chapel within a cathedral'.

THE ROUTE

Like the Coffin Path to Rydal, this route is a popular walk and is best enjoyed as a run in the early morning or, better still, just before sunset, when you can also take advantage of Grasmere's best pub – Tweedies Bar – at the end of your route. Navigation is straightforward as you follow the clearly defined path up to the tarn, keeping the waterfall in sight, then descend right from the tarn. However, the stony paths can be awkward after heavy rain and slow you down on both ascent and descent.

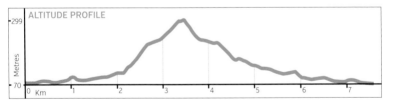

ALTITUDE PROFILE

>> EASEDALE TARN

DISTANCE: 8KM >> *ASCENT:* 219M >> *MAX ALTITUDE:* 299M >> *TYPICAL TIME:* 0:45 HRS >> *TERRAIN:* MOSTLY ROUGH PATHS, SHORT ROAD SECTION >> *NAVIGATION:* STRAIGHTFORWARD >> *START/FINISH:* BROADGATE MEADOW CAR PARK >> *GRID REF:* NY 338077 >> *SATNAV:* LA22 9TA >> *OS MAP:* EXPLORER OL7 THE ENGLISH LAKES SOUTH-EASTERN AREA >> *REFRESHMENTS:* TWEEDIES BAR, GRASMERE TEL: 01539 435 300

DIRECTIONS ≫ EASEDALE TARN

S   Park in the centre of Grasmere and start your run from Easedale Road, following the signs for Easedale Tarn. After just under a mile, when you reach a sharp bend, leave the road and cross over a footbridge to your **left**, passing through a gate and joining the slightly awkward stony track towards Easedale Tarn.

2   **Do not cross** the bridge which you will pass on your right. **Bear left** where the path divides and climb towards the waterfall you can see ahead of you, keeping the stream on your right. The path to Easedale climbs steadily, rocky in places, flattening as you near the top.

3   When you reach the tarn, take the path down to your right and cross the stream by some stepping stones. Bear right again, following the path round a knoll. Your descent soon becomes stony and **care may be required** on this section.

4   As you continue your descent, you should see a large, distinctive rock in the distance. Someone has helpfully painted the word *Grasmere* and an arrow, pointing left. Follow this arrow, **bearing left** on your path. Cross over a footbridge and then **turn right**, taking an easier and flatter track back towards Grasmere.

5   As the track passes beneath Helm Crag, go through the large gate to your **right** and then through a smaller gate soon after. Shortly, this crosses the bridge you passed earlier on the way up to Easedale Tarn. From here, **turn left** and retrace your steps back to the footbridge and Easedale Road. Follow the road back to Grasmere. Easedale Road brings you out conveniently close to Tweedies.

PHIL PICKERING PUSHES ON AT HAYSTACKS

9 ›› HAYSTACKS

8.1km

INTRODUCTION

Of all the Lakeland fells, the great writer and hillwalker Alfred Wainwright chose Haystacks as the place he wanted to have his ashes scattered. Situated at the south-eastern end of the Buttermere valley, it has an interesting, rocky summit and contains a number of attractive tarns and rock formations. Or, as Wainwright himself put it in his *Pictoral Guide to the Lakeland Fells*: 'Haystacks stands unabashed and unashamed in the midst of a circle of much loftier fells.'

THE ROUTE

Short but unforgiving, the climb up to the Haystacks ridge is challenging and steep. Once you gain the top, the path is a bit more tricky underfoot, particularly as you begin to descend. Navigation is a little difficult as you try to find the initial path down, so take care at this point. If you are fit and looking for a tougher challenge, you could run this and then do the route around Buttermere in the same day, using the latter as a warm down (see page 31).

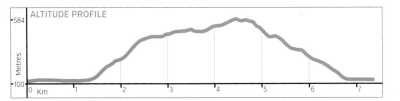

ALTITUDE PROFILE

Metres

584

100

0 Km | 1 | 2 | 3 | 4 | 5 | 6 | 7

›› HAYSTACKS

DISTANCE: 8.1KM ›› *ASCENT:* 510M ›› *MAX ALTITUDE:* 584M ›› *TYPICAL TIME:* 1:10 HRS ›› *TERRAIN:* VERY ROCKY UNDERFOOT IN PLACES ›› *NAVIGATION:* REASONABLY CHALLENGING ›› *START/FINISH:* GATESGARTH FARM ›› *GRID REF:* NY 194150 ›› *SATNAV:* CA13 9XA (NEAREST) ›› *OS MAP:* EXPLORER OL4 THE ENGLISH LAKES NORTH-WESTERN AREA ›› *REFRESHMENTS:* THE FISH INN TEL: 01768 770 253. THERE IS SOMETIMES A SNACK VAN PARKED UP NEAR GATESGARTH FARM TOO.

DIRECTIONS ≫ HAYSTACKS

S   Park at Gatesgarth Farm and walk up the road to Gatesgarth Cottage. Take a track leading **right**, signposted *Public Bridleway*.

2   Follow this track all the way to the first of the high sections of the Haystacks ridge, keeping the river on your right all the way. The way is marked by a series of cairns. Near the top, **ignore the smaller path** crossing the stream off to your right and carry straight on. As it flattens, the path splits into two and you **bear right**; drop down to the stream and cross where you can.

3   This path undulates and zigzags over the top of Haystacks, passing Innominate Tarn on the left, via a series of stone steps which wind up to a summit. There are a number of high points on Haystacks. When you get to the last of these, the path crosses the north end of a little tarn and then doubles back.

4   Follow this path down a very steep and rocky initial descent that leads to Scarth Gap. The route down is awkward underfoot at first and eventually levels off a little, leading all the way back down the hillside. You can see the farm you started from all the while as you descend. Lower down, the track passes above woodland and then turns **sharp right** back towards Gatesgarth Farm. The bridleway left would take you round Buttermere lake, which you could add on as an extra circuit if your legs aren't spent enough.

HELEN MORT ADMIRING THE VIEW AT LOWESWATER

10 >> LOWESWATER

8.6km

INTRODUCTION

Loweswater is one of the smaller Lake District lakes, overlooked by fells including the imposing, distinctive shape of Mellbreak. There's a fell race up the side of Mellbreak each year, but our route doesn't venture into that vertical terrain, instead staying on lower-level paths by the lakeside and through the forest. This is a superb run with varied paths and excellent views all the way.

THE ROUTE

Follow flat paths by the shore of Loweswater all the way out then after crossing a few fields (the farmhouses help with navigation here), return over more undulating ground above the forest with clear views of the lake from above. Springy grass makes for a fast descent where you can let go. Upon returning to Maggie's Bridge, a pint at the Kirkstile Inn in Loweswater is essential.

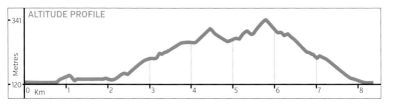

ALTITUDE PROFILE

>> LOWESWATER

DISTANCE: 8.6KM >> *ASCENT:* 287M >> *MAX ALTITUDE:* 341M >> *TYPICAL TIME:* 0:50 HRS >> *TERRAIN:* FOREST TRACKS AND GRASS >> *NAVIGATION:* STRAIGHTFORWARD >> *START/FINISH:* MAGGIE'S BRIDGE CAR PARK, LOWESWATER >> *GRID REF:* NY 134210 >> *SATNAV:* CA13 0RU >> *OS MAP:* EXPLORER OL4 THE ENGLISH LAKES NORTH-WESTERN AREA >> *REFRESHMENTS:* THE KIRKSTILE INN TEL: 01900 85219

DIRECTIONS >> LOWESWATER

S Park at Maggie's Bridge. Cross the cattle grid and follow the track out past the farm, where you take the bridleway **right** and through a gate to Holme Wood.

2 Follow the lakeside track near the shore. After crossing a small bridge, take a track which goes slightly to the **left**, away from the shore. Cross another bridge and pass through a gate. The path returns to the lakeside for a while, and leads you on to Hudson Place.

3 At Hudson Place, **turn right** at the road and **then left** through a gate signposted *Fangs*. Follow this path on through fields to Jenkinson Place and Iredale farm. Keep Iredale on your right and **fork left**, climbing a hill. At the brow of the hill, follow a signpost left to High Nook.

4 The path now climbs up the hill following the wall, then crosses to the left of it after a gate and stile. Take the leftmost track, following a blue arrow on the stile. An excellent stretch of good, downhill running on soft, forgiving grass.

5 After crossing a beck, contour round the forest, keeping it on your left. After the end of the forest, the path continues towards a waterfall and then loops round left after crossing a stream. This takes you through High Nook farm and then back to Maggie's Bridge.

MIROSLAV HALAMICEK FOLLOWS THE COFFIN PATH

11 » COFFIN PATH & RYDAL ROUND   8.7km

INTRODUCTION

A steady, undulating introduction to the world of Lake District trail running. This is an excellent route early in the morning or in the late evening when the tourists disappear and the true atmosphere of the historic corpse road can be appreciated. Our start and finish is Dove Cottage, home to the poet William Wordsworth who liked to compose his verses on the move (though not on the run). At the end of this route we pass St Oswald's church, where the Wordsworth family are buried.

THE ROUTE

This run follows the coffin path out of Grasmere to Rydal before taking in Rydal Water and Grasmere lake. There's a sharp initial climb, then a more gentle up-and-down to Rydal Hall through a series of gates. Once you reach the shores of Rydal and then Grasmere lake, there's faster, flatter running to be had and the final stretch into Grasmere is on road. If you need an extra incentive on the way back, the Gingerbread Shop in Grasmere village sells legendary gingerbread for some well-deserved post-run fuel.

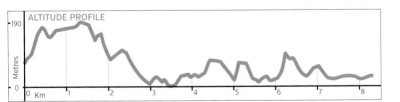

ALTITUDE PROFILE

» **COFFIN PATH & RYDAL ROUND**

DISTANCE: 8.7KM » *ASCENT:* 260M » *MAX ALTITUDE:* 130M » *TYPICAL TIME:* 0:50 HRS » *TERRAIN:* MOSTLY ROUGH PATHS, SHORT ROAD SECTION » *NAVIGATION:* STRAIGHTFORWARD » *START/FINISH:* DOVE COTTAGE/WORDSWORTH TRUST CAR PARK, GRASMERE » *GRID REF:* NY 342069 » *SATNAV:* LA22 9SQ » *OS MAP:* EXPLORER OL7 THE ENGLISH LAKES SOUTH-EASTERN AREA » *REFRESHMENTS:* TWEEDIES BAR, GRASMERE TEL: 01539 435 300

DIRECTIONS ≫ COFFIN PATH & RYDAL ROUND

S Start at the Dove Cottage/Wordsworth Trust car park, just off the A591 outside Grasmere. Leave the car park by the track that leads towards Dove Cottage. With the cottage in front of you, **turn right** on the road, climbing steeply until you reach a turn-off. **Turn left** (signposted *No through road*) – the road to the right leads back down to the A591.

2 As the road continues to climb, you'll see a signpost marked *Coffin Route to Rydal*. This is the route you will be following for the next couple of kilometres. After you pass a large pond then a house on your left, the road becomes a track. Follow this all the way to Rydal, as it narrows and undulates. You will pass through a series of gates at regular intervals, which give the welcome chance for a short breather.

3 Where the track ends, you'll see a sign for Rydal Hall ahead of you. **Turn right** and descend the hill to the A591, keeping Rydal Hall on your left. At the A591, **turn right**. **Cross the road** at the Badger Bar and take the public footpath across the bridge on the other side.

4 After the stile, **turn right**. Follow the path as it contours round Rydal Water, first through some woods, then by the side of the lake.

5 Eventually, this path contours right and climbs steeply. **Keep to the track** and **ignore the gates** on your right. Climb until the view opens out and you overlook Grasmere lake. Follow the narrow path down to the shore.

6 From the shore, pass through a gate and the path turns right through the woods. Enjoy this fast, flat section by the lakeside. It finishes in a short, sharp climb up to Red Bank Road, where you **turn right** and follow the sign back into Grasmere.

7 With the Dale Lodge Hotel on your left and Red Bank Road car park on your right, **turn right** and follow the road back towards the A591 and the Wordsworth Trust car park.

MUDDY PATHS NEAR MELBREAK

12 ›› CRUMMOCK WATER

8.8km

INTRODUCTION

Another superb route from Loweswater offering imposing views and one of the best pubs in the Lake District as a start and finish. If you're after more mileage, you could join this route together with the Loweswater run, since the parking spots are reasonably close together. Crummock Water is flanked by steep fellsides of Skiddaw slate and Alfred Wainwright was moved to say of it, 'No pairing of hill and lake in Lakeland have a closer partnership than these'.

THE ROUTE

The route passes just above the lakeside for most of the way, avoiding the low path which is prone to flooding. All the same, you may find the paths that curve around Mellbreak quite damp underfoot. The track back towards the Kirkstile Inn is fast and flat, and you'll be spurred on by the prospect of Loweswater Gold.

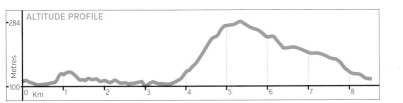

ALTITUDE PROFILE

›› CRUMMOCK WATER

DISTANCE: 8.8KM ›› *ASCENT:* 226M ›› *MAX ALTITUDE:* 284M ›› *TYPICAL TIME:* 1 HR ›› *TERRAIN:* STONY TRACKS AND GRASS. CAN BE BOGGY IN PLACES ›› *NAVIGATION:* STRAIGHTFORWARD ›› *START/FINISH:* THE KIRKSTILE INN, LOWESWATER ›› *GRID REF:* NY 141209 ›› *SATNAV:* CA13 0RU ›› *OS MAP:* EXPLORER OL4 THE ENGLISH LAKES NORTH-WESTERN AREA ›› *REFRESHMENTS:* THE KIRKSTILE INN TEL: 01900 85219

DIRECTIONS >> CRUMMOCK WATER

S Park either at the Kirkstile Inn or just over the bridge next to the pub. From the Inn, follow a sign that says *No road to the lake*.

2 At a fork, **turn right** – the road has a dead end sign here and you follow straight on as it becomes a track, ignoring smaller paths to left and right. Pass a house on your right and go through a gate to the start of the grassy trail, **turning almost immediately right** up the hill and passing through a gate signed *Crummock and Buttermere*.

3 Your path is elevated above Crummock Water for a long stretch. Eventually this joins the path by the lakeside.

4 Not long after passing High Ling and Low Ling you reach a bridge. **Turn right just before it** and climb the grassy path keeping the stream on your left, passing several bridges as you climb steadily.

5 The path veers away from the stream after a third bridge and climbs more steeply. Approximately 4.8 kilometres into your run, you reach a fence. **Turn right**, keeping the fence left. At the next fence take the stile and **fork left**.

6 This path takes you round Mellbreak through the Mosedale valley. It starts off boggy, then becomes grassy and finally turns into a good track which takes you all the way back to the Kirkstile Inn.

HELEN MORT ABOVE GRASMERE LAKE AFTER THE DESCENT FROM LOUGHRIGG

13 >> LOUGHRIGG

10km

INTRODUCTION

If you want to leave the low trails but your legs aren't ready for the high ridges yet, this route is a nice, moderate introduction to steeper terrain. Loughrigg is surrounded by an unusual amount of open water (and, running in a typical Lakeland summer, you may find yourself drenched by an unusual amount too). From the summit, you can see Grasmere lake and Windermere as well as the Langdale Pikes and Fairfield Horseshoe.

THE ROUTE

This run starts and finishes in Ambleside, and there's a nice warm-up on the flat through Rothay Park. There are a series of paths running up to the summit of Loughrigg in places and, as long as you've started on the right track when you reach the fellside, many lead to the same place (some boggier than others!). In wet conditions, the paved descent down to Loughrigg Terrace can be slippery and you might even prefer to run the route in reverse, starting out along Under Loughrigg Road. The paths along Loughrigg Terrace and down past Rydal Caves are good for speed merchants. If you can still bear the thought of another small hill after you finish, the Golden Rule at the foot of The Struggle is a good destination and a short walk or run from Rothay Park.

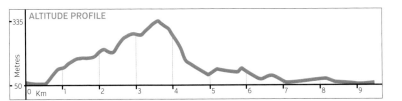

ALTITUDE PROFILE

Metres — 335 / 50

0 Km 1 2 3 4 5 6 7 8 9

>> LOUGHRIGG

DISTANCE: 10KM >> *ASCENT:* 381M >> *MAX ALTITUDE:* 335M >> *TYPICAL TIME:* 1:10 HRS >> *TERRAIN:* GRASSY PATHS, TRACKS, SHORT TARMAC SECTION >> *NAVIGATION:* MODERATE >> *START/FINISH:* AMBLESIDE
GRID REF: NY 375044 >> *SATNAV:* LA22 9DJ >> *OS MAP:* EXPLORER OL7 THE ENGLISH LAKES, SOUTH-EASTERN AREA >> *REFRESHMENTS:* GOLDEN RULE, AMBLESIDE TEL: 01539 432 257

DIRECTIONS » LOUGHRIGG

S Park in Ambleside and start your run from outside Zefirellis cinema. Follow the sign to Rothay Park and Loughrigg. At the end of the park, **turn left** over a bridge and then cross a cattle grid. Shortly after this, the road divides: **bear left**, over another cattle grid.

2 Follow this road as it climbs up to Loughrigg and – after passing through a gate – becomes a track. At the last gate before the fellside, a slate sign directs you onwards for Loughrigg, Langdale and Elterwater.

3 Follow the track as it bears round to the left. After a series of small stepping stones, **fork right** and begin your undulating climb to the top of the fell. Some sections are steep and rocky, others flatter and more open. You are aiming for a small notch on the skyline. Where the path splits keep heading for the notch. Climb to a col below a cairn and **bear right** and **then left** around a boggy patch and sometimes tarn. The trig point on the summit should come into view slightly left and still much higher.

4 There are several paths that cross the plateau top and lead to the summit. Keep aiming for the trig point.

5 From the summit trig point, **bear right** and begin your descent, north-west towards Dunmail Raise. The path down is rocky and steep in places and sometimes there's easier running on the grass on either side. As you descend, you get fine views of Grasmere lake.

6 When you reach the large path at Loughrigg Terrace, **turn sharply right** and follow the path right across the fellside to its obvious end. **Bear right** on to a path crossing the shoulder of a small knoll below Ewe Crag. Climb the shoulder and run down the other side to the permissive path to Rydal Cave.

7 From Rydal Cave, take the path **left** as it zigzags down the hill and then flattens out, keeping high above Rydal Water on your left.

8 When you reach the gate at the end of the track, pass through it and carry on down the lane. Keep going past the cottages and on to Pelter Bridge.

9   Don't take the bridge, **turn right** and join Under Loughrigg Road which leads you all
the way back to Rothay Park. On returning to Rothay Park, retrace your earlier route
and turn **left** as you leave the park.

MATTHEW BUTLER ENJOYING THE DOWNHILL AT GRISEDALE

INTRODUCTION

Above Patterdale, Grisedale Beck flows from Grisedale Tarn, nestled high between the fells of Fairfield, Seat Sandal and Dollywaggon Pike. This run affords views of St Sunday Crag and Helvellyn too and there's a grandeur to the valley even on a misty day. There's the option of extending this run out to Lanty's Tarn if you like on the way back – carry straight on instead of turning right through the gate at Brownend and loop high around the tarn.

THE ROUTE

Follow good tracks on the way out, until you get close to the turning point when the track steepens and there's some loose rock underfoot. The way back is much faster and easier. At the end of the run, you can either return to Patterdale by road if you want to get some speed up or retrace the route you took in the very early part of the run if you'd prefer another glimpse of the view over to Ullswater.

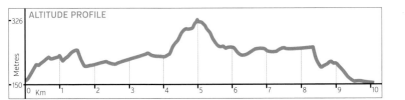

ALTITUDE PROFILE

Metres

326

150

0   Km   1   2   3   4   5   6   7   8   9   10

» GRISEDALE

DISTANCE: 10.4KM » *ASCENT:* 297M » *MAX ALTITUDE:* 326M » *TYPICAL TIME:* 1:10 HRS
TERRAIN: FOOTPATHS » *NAVIGATION:* MODERATELY EASY » *START/FINISH:* PATTERDALE HOTEL
GRID REF: NY 396159 » *SATNAV:* CA11 0NN » *OS MAP:* EXPLORER OL5 THE ENGLISH LAKES NORTH-EASTERN AREA » *REFRESHMENTS:* PATTERDALE HOTEL TEL: 01768 482 231

DIRECTIONS >> GRISEDALE

S   Park near the Patterdale Hotel and take the public footpath signposted at the back of the hotel buildings, passing through a gate soon after. When you reach another gate on your right, pass through it and take the track.

2   After crossing a beck, Ullswater reveals itself and makes for a distracting, lovely view. Continue on this track and at a rectangular stone enclosure, **turn right** following an arrow. **Turn left** when you reach the private road. This turns into a track which follows the river.

3   After the last forest plantation on your right, the path starts to climb and you head up towards Ruthwaite Lodge. As you get higher, the path levels and gets easier underfoot and you will see a bridge ahead of you which you cross for the return leg (you cross another bridge before this but there is no choice of paths). If you reach the lodge, you have gone too far!

4   Run back along the valley on good paths. By a wall, **just before** you reach Brownend plantation, **turn right** through the gate and drop down to the road which crosses the stream. **Turn left** and follow the road back to Patterdale. If you'd prefer to avoid the road, you can **turn right** instead and go up the hill to rejoin the path you followed at the start of your run.

LUCA JANDU TAKING ONE OF THE MANY PATHS ACROSS ASKHAM FELL

15 ›› ASKHAM FELL

10.5km

INTRODUCTION

Askham is an attractive village near Penrith, adjoining the River Lowther. This run offers an easy, varied and mostly flat route which takes you away from the crowds that swarm the central Lakes. Well worth the journey. If you're coming from the south, your drive in will probably take you along the beautiful shores of Ullswater, through Pooley Bridge.

THE ROUTE

The path out is along Askham Fell, which can feel surprisingly remote and offers splendid isolation on the right day. Your return journey takes in a riverside path and a woodland stretch on great tracks. Easy underfoot all the way.

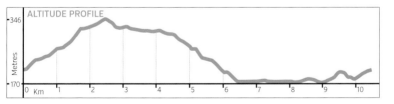

›› ASKHAM FELL

DISTANCE: 10.5KM ›› **ASCENT:** 170M ›› **MAX ALTITUDE:** 346M ›› **TYPICAL TIME:** 1 HR ›› **TERRAIN:** FOOTPATHS, GRASS ›› **NAVIGATION:** SLIGHTLY FIDDLY IN PLACES, BUT MANY OF THE EARLY PATHS LEAD TO THE SAME PLACE ›› **START/FINISH:** THE QUEENS HEAD, ASKHAM ›› **GRID REF:** NY 396159 ›› **SATNAV:** CA10 2PF **OS MAP:** EXPLORER OL5 THE ENGLISH LAKES NORTH-EASTERN AREA ›› **REFRESHMENTS:** THE QUEENS HEAD, ASKHAM TEL: 01931 712 225

DIRECTIONS ≫ ASKHAM FELL

S Start from The Queens Head in Askham, where there is free parking. **Turn left** out of the car park and take the first road on the **right**, past the pottery. **Continue straight on** up the **right fork**, signposted as a dead end. This becomes a steady climb out towards Askham Fell. At the cattle grid, continue to **bear right**.

2 After about a mile and a half from Askham, you reach a distinctive rectangle of woodland on your right – **bear left** here down towards Ketley Gate. There are several tracks crossing the fell side and all of them will eventually lead back to the Ketley Gate path. At the gatepost, take the track which doubles back towards the village of Helton.

3 As you run downhill on the excellent track, you pass some clumps of trees close by on the left. **Look out for a standing stone**, also on your left. Here, **bear left** and soon arrive at an unfenced road. A small fingerpost points across to Setterah Park. **Follow this** and continue downhill towards Helton, over a stile and across several fields.

4 The right of way crosses to the bottom left-hand corner of the first narrow paddock, then follows a wall to the bottom of the next field. You then follow an overgrown walled path – **very briefly** for about 20 yards – and take a squeezer gate on your **left**. Go through this and cross the fields, aiming for a house with a conservatory in front of you.

5 After a ladder stile, **turn left** and diagonally beyond this, reach a lane. Follow the signed bridleway marked *Whale* down a small green lane towards the River Lowther.

6 When you reach a wide footbridge, don't cross the bridge but **turn sharply left** and stay close to the river for a stretch, following it downstream.

7 When you reach the road, **turn right**, cross the river and go **left** through a green and white gate, joining a permitted path north through the Lowther estate. This eventually leads through another distinctive green and white gate into woodland, and shortly after this you take the **left fork** back towards the road that leads (uphill and left) to Askham.

© CROWN COPYRIGHT AND/OR DATABASE RIGHT. ALL RIGHTS RESERVED. LICENCE NUMBER 100025218.

16 >> ENNERDALE

11.6km

INTRODUCTION

Ennerdale is the only Lake District lake that does not have a road running alongside it, so you can run around the perimeter flanked by heather on one shore and forest on the other. It is a deep glacial lake, two and a half miles long, and its clear waters contain a variety of fish which you sometimes glimpse as you run past (if you have time to look!).

THE ROUTE

One of the most easy to navigate of the Lakes' trail runs, it's hard to go wrong as you follow the paths around Ennerdale. On the way out, the going can be quite rough underfoot and you might have to force yourself to look at your feet from time to time instead of the fine views of Great Gable, Green Gable, Temple and Pillar. The section over Anglers' Crag requires particular care. The route back is less interesting for the first stretch along a forest track (watch out for occasional cars) but is fast and flat, allowing you to stride out. You return to the shore and views near the end as you return towards the car park.

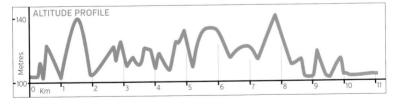

>> **ENNERDALE**

DISTANCE: 11.6KM >> *ASCENT:* 131M >> *MAX ALTITUDE:* 140M >> *TYPICAL TIME:* 1:20 HRS >> *TERRAIN:* ROCKY LAKESIDE TRACKS, SMOOTH SURFACED TRACKS >> *NAVIGATION:* EASY >> *START/FINISH:* BLEACH GREEN CAR PARK, ENNERDALE >> *GRID REF:* NY 085153 >> *SATNAV:* CA23 3AS >> *OS MAP:* EXPLORER OL4 THE ENGLISH LAKES NORTH-WESTERN AREA >> *REFRESHMENTS:* THE FOX AND HOUNDS, ENNERDALE BRIDGE TEL: 01946 861 373

DIRECTIONS >> ENNERDALE

S   Park at Bleach Green car park and leave through a gate at the back of the parking area.

2   Continue past a mountain rescue donation box along a stony track and **bear right** when you reach the weir. The path you join here takes you to the end of the lake – it is undulating and stony underfoot, and has a few rocky sections in places, particularly over Anglers' Crag.

3   At the end of the lake pass through a gate, cross a stream and follow an obvious grassy track away from the lake, following yellow waymarkers. Reach a bigger track and a parking spot. **Turn left** here and run towards the forest.

4   Just before the forest, cross a bridge. **Turn left** and follow the forest track along the lake shore, watching out for traffic in places. A fast, flat section with occasional glimpses of the lake.

5   At Bowness Knot car park, leave the track and follow a public footpath signed for Bleach Green, keeping to the lakeside all the way. This brings you back out by a bridge and the weir you passed at the start of the run. **Turn right** to return to Bleach Green car park.

LEAP OF FAITH: THE ROCKY PATHS ABOVE ULLSWATER

13.1km

INTRODUCTION

At nine miles long, Ullswater is the second largest lake in the Lake District. There's a pleasant run along the eastern shore to Howtown, returning by the ferry, but this route offers a more challenging variation, returning via Place Fell. Your reward is a vista including Helvellyn, St Sunday Crag and Fairfield, and a great descent back into Patterdale.

THE ROUTE

A steady, mostly flat section at the start of the run contours around the shore of Ullswater on good tracks. The return to Patterdale is much steeper, with some respite as you near Place Fell. There are a few paths across these fells, but the easiest route is by the most obvious, well-worn track. The descent path is good and fast in places. Route finding is mostly straightforward, though care is required in a few places as you climb towards High Knott, Mortar Crag and The Knight.

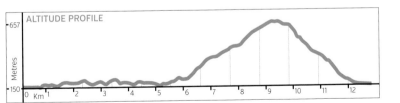

ALTITUDE PROFILE

657 / Metres / 150

0 Km 1 2 3 4 5 6 7 8 9 10 11 12

» **PLACE FELL & ULLSWATER**

DISTANCE: 13.1KM » *ASCENT:* 603M » *MAX ALTITUDE:* 657M » *TYPICAL TIME:* 1:45 HRS » *TERRAIN:* ROCKY FOOTPATHS, GRASSY TRACKS » *NAVIGATION:* MODERATE » *START/FINISH:* PATTERDALE HOTEL *GRID REF:* NY 396159 » *SATNAV:* CA11 0NN » *OS MAP:* EXPLORER OL5 THE ENGLISH LAKES NORTH-EASTERN AREA » *REFRESHMENTS:* PATTERDALE HOTEL TEL: 01768 482 231

DIRECTIONS » PLACE FELL & ULLSWATER

S   Park opposite the Patterdale Hotel and **turn right** on to the main road. Take a track to your **right** just beyond the school, signposted *Boredale* and *Howtown*.

2   When you reach a farm, go through it and **turn left**, taking the track that runs towards the lake shore. Stick to this track – you have the option of a higher path at one point which rejoins the lower track later on.

3   After about 5.6 kilometres, you will see Scalehow Force waterfall above you on the right, then cross a footbridge. A little beyond this, you reach another stream and see a stone building in front of you. Take the grassy track before the stream that doubles back to climb towards High Knott.

4   Your path climbs the fells above Ullswater, passing a disused quarry on the way. After 7.6 kilometres, the path becomes more indistinct and divides. **Take the right fork** that runs **due west** towards a sheepfold and up towards Mortar Crag.

5   As you pass over the fells, keep to the most distinct track all the way to Place Fell. Near the summit of Place Fell, pass a tarn on your left and climb past the trig point.

6   The descent from Place Fell is quite steep and is paved with stones in places. At a dip, you see the path ahead rising towards Stony Rigg. At the junction of paths at Boredale Hause, **turn right**, descending past the cairn towards Patterdale.

7   Where the path forks, **keep right**. The path brings you out to a gate, which you pass through and **turn left**, taking a small road back towards the main road. At the main road, **turn right** back towards the hotel.

Lake District National Park

Cumbrian Mountains

ALICJA ZASUCHA DESCENDING TOWARDS HAWESWATER

18 » HAWESWATER

14.8km

INTRODUCTION

If you have the time to drive a little further north on the M6, it is well worth the journey to tranquil Haweswater for this rewarding circuit which includes a section on an old coffin route. The run doesn't go up on to the tops of the fells, but you still get a lot of elevation and great views, and you may be lucky enough to see stags or red squirrels. The Old Corpse Road links the isolated hamlet of Swindale Head in Mosedale with Mardale. It's a bleak but beautiful crossing, with views to High Street and Harter Fell. If you do this route at a less popular time of year, you may not see a single other person on your way round once you leave Gatescarth Pass.

THE ROUTE

This is a beautiful, longer route that offers splendid isolation and fine views of Haweswater from above. The initial climb over to Gatescarth Pass is testing but easy underfoot. The section towards Mosedale and Swindale may be boggy in places. Navigation is most difficult from Swindale to Mardale where the track can be very unclear and for this reason you shouldn't attempt this run in poor visibility or with bad conditions forecast, particularly as this route is so remote. The final section involves a stretch on the road, but with Haweswater on your right and little traffic, you hardly notice.

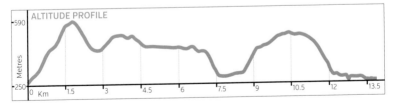

» HAWESWATER

DISTANCE: 14.8KM » **ASCENT:** 681M » **MAX ALTITUDE:** 590M » **TYPICAL TIME:** 2:15 HRS
TERRAIN: ROCKY FOOTPATHS, GRASSY TRACKS, SHORT ROAD SECTION » **NAVIGATION:** MODERATE
START/FINISH: CAR PARK, HAWESWATER » **GRID REF:** NY 469107 » **SATNAV:** CA10 2RP (NEAREST)
OS MAP: EXPLORER OL5 THE ENGLISH LAKES NORTH-EASTERN AREA » **REFRESHMENTS:** HAWESWATER HOTEL TEL: 01931 713 232

DIRECTIONS >> HAWESWATER

S From the car park, take the track opposite (signposted *Gatescarth Pass*) and climb steeply with Harter Fell to your right and a stream to your left. At the top of the climb, you reach a fence. **Ignore** the path to the right which leads up the fell and **carry straight on** through a gate. The path begins a rapid descent.

2 As the descent levels off, **turn left** off the track, following a sign for *Swindale Head*. Cross the beck and follow the path towards an indistinct shoulder.

3 This path traverses towards Mosedale with the beck on your right. Eventually, Mosedale Cottage comes into view. Ford a stream immediately after the cottage and carry on to another ford. After this second ford, take an **indistinct left fork** in the path and climb slightly away from the beck.

4 Follow this path as it descends into Swindale and towards the few houses of Swindale Head. After the cottages, follow a signpost to *Mardale via the Corpse Road*.

5 The path climbs directly up the hillside for a couple of hundred metres and then, crossing a stream, does a single long zigzag to cross the same stream again 50m or so higher up. Until the descent into Mardale this is the last time the path looks constructed. After this point, it is a faint line in the grass and may be hard to follow. **Take care** on these kilometres across the fell, looking out for landmarks like Rowantreethwaite cairn on your right and **ignoring** a more distinct track on your left that leads up over steeper fells.

6 Eventually, the path begins a steep, zigzag descent back into Haweswater. When you reach the road, **turn left** to return to the car park.

THE PUNISHING TRACK OVER THE GATESCARTH PASS

MIROSLAV HALAMICEK STARTING UP THE FIRST HILL OF THE FAIRFIELD HORSESHOE

19 >> FAIRFIELD HORSESHOE 16.8km

INTRODUCTION

A challenging circuit of the fells with superb views from the ridge on a clear day, this classic walking route is a good run to try once your legs have acclimatised to the Lakeland terrain. Alfred Wainwright was slightly dismissive of Fairfield from the south, noting that, 'It appears as a great horseshoe of grassy slopes below a consistently high skyline ... but lacking those dramatic qualities that appeal most to the lover of hills'. After you've run from Nab Scar, however, the long but gentle slopes of Fairfield are a welcome reprieve.

THE ROUTE

I suggest starting in Rydal, getting stuck in to the steep ground straight away, but you could also run from the main car park in Ambleside if you prefer a steadier section before the first big climb. From Nab Scar, the ridge undulates more gently and the paths on the way up to Fairfield are usually good underfoot. In good weather the ridge is obvious, but in poor visibility, the Fairfield and Hart Crag section of the route can be tricky to navigate and it's worth pausing your run to make sure you're taking the right line down – the wall becomes your guide in the last section. If you go wrong, you might end up in Patterdale, trying to hitch a lift back over the Kirkstone Pass!

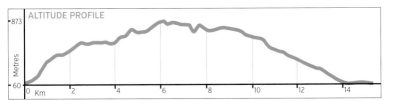

>> FAIRFIELD HORSESHOE

DISTANCE: 16.8KM >> *ASCENT:* 1080M >> *MAX ALTITUDE:* 873M >> *TYPICAL TIME:* 2:30 HRS
TERRAIN: GRASSY PATHS AND TRACKS, OFTEN MUDDY >> *NAVIGATION:* CAN BE VERY DIFFICULT IN POOR VISIBILITY >> *START/FINISH:* RYDAL CHURCH >> *GRID REF:* NY 364061 >> *SATNAV:* LA22 9LX
OS MAP: EXPLORER OL7 THE ENGLISH LAKES SOUTH-EASTERN AREA >> *REFRESHMENTS:* GLEN ROTHAY HOTEL AND BADGER BAR TEL: 01539 434 500

DIRECTIONS >> FAIRFIELD HORSESHOE

S Start from Rydal church, where there is usually all-day parking available for a small donation. Climb steeply up the hill, keeping Rydal Hall on your right. The road bears slightly to the left behind Rydal Mount and – after a small gate – becomes a track which climbs to the top of Nab Scar, your first peak.

2 From Nab Scar, with its fine view back to Rydal Water, continue north to Heron Pike and Great Rigg along the high crest. This section can be boggy in places.

3 Climb steadily up the stony dome which leads to the summit of Fairfield – there are many cairns along the way.

4 Follow the path in an easterly direction, then south-east towards Hart Crag. At the top of Hart Crag the path levels out and there is a large cairn. Avoid the obvious path that descends from the cairn (down into Patterdale) and **bear right** instead, taking a less-clear path over stony ground. After a rocky descent, the path soon starts to run alongside a collapsed stone wall, which guides your way almost all the way back to Ambleside.

5 Follow the wall as it runs over High Pike and Low Pike. The path to the left of it is often easier for running. Eventually, you come out into a wooded valley overlooking Scandale Beck. You meet a farm road that leads to Low Sweden Bridge and Nook End Farm, taking you into Ambleside via minor roads. (Alternatively, you can head west before Low Sweden Bridge and join the track to Rydal Hall and Rydal Mount.)

6 From the village centre, take the A591 towards Grasmere. After the last of the houses, cross a small bridge. Turn **right** along a track through stone gateposts and follow the public footpath sign that points back to Rydal Hall.

MATTHEW BUTLER WISHES HE BROUGHT SPARE SOCKS AT TROUTBECK

20 ≫ TROUTBECK ROUND

17km

INTRODUCTION

A challenging, increasingly exhilarating route which takes in part of the majestic Kentmere round. Rather than starting from Kentmere (where parking is notoriously difficult), this run begins from the historic village of Troutbeck, where sunlight through the church windows filters through striking stained glass in the Pre-Raphaelite style.

THE ROUTE

The track out from Troutbeck is deceptively flat (if a bit wet in places – you may want to bring a spare pair of socks!). The climb up to Park Fell corrects that – a steep and direct stretch up to the ridge, where you're rewarded with the view over to Kentmere Reservoir and High Street. The undulating track back over three summits is excellent and about as easy underfoot as anything you'll find in the Lakeland fells.

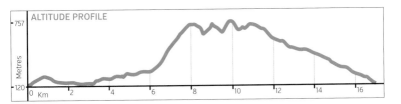

ALTITUDE PROFILE

≫ **TROUTBECK ROUND**

DISTANCE: 17KM ≫ *ASCENT:* 850M ≫ *MAX ALTITUDE:* 757M ≫ *TYPICAL TIME:* 2 HRS ≫ *TERRAIN:* GRASSY PATHS AND TRACKS, OFTEN MUDDY ≫ *NAVIGATION:* MODERATE ≫ *START/FINISH:* TROUTBECK VILLAGE *GRID REF:* NY 412027 ≫ *SATNAV:* LA23 1PF ≫ *OS MAP:* EXPLORER OL7 THE ENGLISH LAKES SOUTH-EASTERN AREA ≫ *REFRESHMENTS:* THE MORTAL MAN, TROUTBECK TEL: 01539 433 193

DIRECTIONS » TROUTBECK ROUND

S Park near the church in the village of Troutbeck (there are quite a few spaces for cars just over the bridge). To start your run, follow the footpath at the side of the A592 **south** towards Windermere for about 150m. Take the bridleway on your **left** signposted *Kentmere* and follow it as it climbs out of the village, past The Howe on your left.

2 Not much further on, you will see the Garburn Pass track climbing steeply to your right. This is where your descent finishes at the end of your run. For now, you **take the left fork** of the path instead and descend for a while, passing a static caravan site on your left.

3 The path out towards Park Fell is relatively flat and enjoys fine views, but it can be somewhat damp underfoot depending on conditions – be prepared for feet wet on this route. A few kilometres in, cross a ford (which could present a challenge after really heavy rainfall).

4 Pass The Tongue on your left. The path joins with Ing Lane and begins to gradually climb towards Park Fell. As it steepens, the track leads towards a gate on the fell side. After the gate, follow the path keeping the wall on your immediate left for 400m. The path then forks and you **bear right** towards the summit of Park Fell, beginning the first steep climb of your run.

5 By the (5-mile) halfway point of the run, you reach a high point on Park Fell and double back along the clearly defined path which takes you to the summit of Froswick, then Ill Bell (the summit marked with a series of cairns) and then Yoke. This track is excellent underfoot and the elevation gives good views of Kentmere Reservoir and Windermere.

6 The descent from Yoke eventually meets the Garburn Pass track: **fork right**, back towards Troutbeck. After 1.5km, you will come out at the fork in the path described at the beginning of this route. **Fork right** and then retrace your steps back to the main road and **turn right** back towards the village.

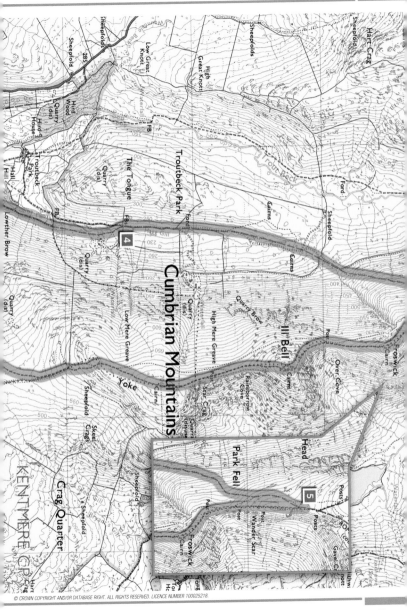

>> APPENDIX

The following is a list of Tourist Information Centres, shops, cafes, pubs, websites and other contacts that might come in handy.

Cumbria Tourism . . . . *www.golakes.co.uk*

Official website of the **Lake District National Park** . . . . *www.lakedistrict.gov.uk*

Ambleside, Central Buildings, Market Cross
T 0844 225 0544 . . . **E** tic@thehubofambleside.com

Coniston, Ruskin Avenue . . . . **T** 01539 441 533
E mail@conistontic.org . . . . . . *www.conistontic.org*

Grasmere, Red Bank Road . . . . **T** 01539 435 245

Kendal, Made in Cumbria, Stramongate
T 01539 735 891 . . . . **E** info@kendaltic.com

Keswick, Market Square . . . . **T** 01768 775 043
E keswicktic@lakedistrict.gov.uk

Penrith . . . . **T** 01768 867 466
E pen.tic@eden.gov.uk . . . . *www.visiteden.co.uk*

Seatoller, Borrowdale . . . . **T** 01768 777 294

Ullswater, Beckside Car Park, Glenridding
T 01768 482 414 . . **E** ullswatertic@lakedistrict.gov.uk

Windermere, Glebe Road . . . . **T** 01539 488 005
E BownessTIC@lakedistrict.gov.uk

FOOD AND DRINK
CAFES
(See individual routes for recommendations.)

Shepherd's 'Caff', High Lodore Farm, Borrowdale

Wilf's, Staveley . . . . **T** 01539 822 329
www.wilfs-cafe.co.uk

Bluebird Cafe, Coniston . . . . **T** 01539 441 649
www.thebluebirdcafe.co.uk

The Old Sawmill Tearoom,
Mirehouse . . . . **T** 01768 774 317

Chesters, Skelwith Bridge . . . . **T** 01539 434 711
www.chestersbytheriver.co.uk

Fellbites, Glenridding . . . . **T** 01768 482 781
www.fellbitescafe.co.uk

Rydal Hall Tea Room, Rydal . . . . . . **T** 01539 432 050

Bilbo's Cafe, Ambleside . . . . **T** 01539 433 660
www.bilboscafe.co.uk

Baldry's Tearoom, Grasmere . . . . . . **T** 01539 435 301
www.baldryscottage.co.uk

Cafe Altitude, Ambleside . . . . **T** 07507 719 202
www.amblesideadventure.co.uk

Apple Pie Eating House,
Ambleside . . . . **T** 01539 433 679
www.applepieambleside.co.uk

PUBS
(See individual routes for recommendations.)

Tweedies Bar, Grasmere . . . . **T** 01539 435 300
www.dalelodgehotel.co.uk/tweedies-bar

The Haweswater Hotel . . . . **T** 01931 713 235
www.haweswaterhotel.com

Kirkstile Inn, Loweswater . . . . **T** 01900 85219
www.kirkstile.com

**The Glen Rothay Hotel and
Badger Bar**, Rydal . . . . **T** 01539 434 500
www.theglenrothay.co.uk/the-badger-bar

The Britannia, Elterwater . . . . **T** 01539 437 210
www.thebritanniainn.com

Golden Rule, Ambleside . . . . **T** 01539 432 257
www.goldenrule-ambleside.co.uk

Old Dungeon Ghyll Hotel,
Great Langdale . . . . **T** 01539 437 272
www.odg.co.uk

The Mill Inn, Mungrisdale . . . . **T** 01768 779 632
www.the-millinn.co.uk

Travellers Rest, Glenridding . . . . **T** 01768 482 298

The Wasdale Head Inn . . . . **T** 01946 726 229
www.wasdale.com

Wainwrights' Inn, Chapel Stile . . . **T** 01539 438 088
www.langdale.co.uk

ACCOMMODATION

YOUTH HOSTELS

YHA youth hostels can be found in the following places. For more information please visit www.yha.org.uk

Ambleside	**T** 0845 371 9620
Borrowdale	**T** 0845 371 9624
Coniston (Coppermines)	**T** 0845 371 9630
Grasmere (Butharlyp Howe)	**T** 0845 371 9319
Helvellyn	**T** 0845 371 9742
Keswick	**T** 0845 371 9746
Langdale	**T** 01539 437 579
Skiddaw House	**T** 07747 174 293
Wasdale Hall	**T** 0845 371 9350
Windermere	**T** 0845 371 9352

BUNKHOUSES, B&BS AND HOTELS

www.staylakedistrict.co.uk
For specific information, contact a Tourist Information Centre in the area in which you intend to stay.

CAMPING

Wasdale Head Campsite, Wasdale .... **T** 01946 726 220
www.nationaltrust.org.uk

Chapel House Farm Campsite, Borrowdale .... **T** 01768 777 256
www.chapelhousefarmcampsite.co.uk

Great Langdale, Langdale .... **T** 01539 437 668
www.nationaltrust.org.uk

There are many more campsites in the Lake District – try www.coolcamping.co.uk or www.golakes.co.uk

WEATHER

www.metoffice.gov.uk .... www.mwis.org.uk

RUNNING & OUTDOOR SHOPS

Pete Bland Sports, Kendal .... **T** 01539 731 012
www.peteblandsports.co.uk

Rock + Run (online) .... **T** 01539 564 540
www.rockrun.com

The Climbers Shop, Ambleside .... **T** 01539 430 122
www.climbers-shop.com

Needle Sports, Keswick .... **T** 01768 772 227
www.needlesports.com

George Fisher Ltd .... **T** 01768 772 178
www.georgefisher.co.uk

planetFear, Keswick .... **T** 01768 800 504
www.planetfear.com

The Epicentre, Ambleside .... **T** 01539 528 528
www.theepicentre.co.uk

Cotswold Outdoor, Keswick, Grasmere and Ambleside .... www.cotswoldoutdoor.com

Stewart Cunningham, Ambleside
T 01539 432 636 .... www.srcunningham.co.uk

The Barn Door Shop, Wasdale Head
T 01946 726 384 .... www.barndoorshop.co.uk

Freetime, Carlisle www.freetime1.co.uk

Nevisport, Kendal .... **T** 01539 734 428
www.nevisport.com

Outdoor@Rheged, Rheged Centre
T 01768 860 046 .... www.rheged.com

Adventure Peaks, Ambleside .... **T** 01539 433 794
www.adventurepeaks.com

OTHER PUBLICATIONS

Good Run Guide
Louise Piears & Andy Bickerstaff
Vertebrate Publishing .... www.v-publishing.co.uk

Peak District Trail Running
Nikalas Cook & Jon Barton
Vertebrate Publishing .... www.v-publishing.co.uk

North Wales Trail Running (2017)
Steve Franklin
Vertebrate Publishing .... www.v-publishing.co.uk

Day Walks in the Lake District
Stephen Goodwin
Vertebrate Publishing .... www.v-publishing.co.uk

Lake District Climbs and Scrambles
Stephen Goodwin
Vertebrate Publishing .... www.v-publishing.co.uk

Lake District Mountain Biking
Richard Staton & Chris Gore
Vertebrate Publishing .... www.v-publishing.co.uk

ABOUT THE AUTHOR

Helen Mort is a writer, trail runner and climber who lives in Sheffield. She has been running since the age of 12, competing on the track, roads and fells over every distance from steeplechase to the marathon. Helen has represented Yorkshire for cross-country. In 2015, she ran her first sub-three-hour marathon, a success she attributes to years of trail running in Derbyshire and the Lake District, where she was a proud member of Ambleside AC.

ABOUT THE PHOTOGRAPHER

Jan Bella is a Slovakian-born photographer, keen traveller and climber living in the Lake District. His ambition to capture people's portraits in the landscapes that inspire them has taken him to India, the Himalaya and Ethiopia. His photographs of Varanasi were featured in the 'Utopian Cities' project. *www.janbellaphotographer.com*

ABOUT VERTEBRATE PUBLISHING

At Vertebrate Publishing we publish books to inspire adventure.

It's our rule that the only books we publish are those that we'd want to read or use ourselves. We endeavour to bring you beautiful books that stand the test of time and that you'll be proud to have on your bookshelf for years to come.

The Peak District was the inspiration behind our first books. Our offices are situated on its doorstep, minutes away from world-class climbing, biking and hillwalking. We're driven by our own passion for the outdoors, for exploration, and for the natural world; it's this passion that we want to share with our readers.

We aim to inspire everyone to get out there. We want to connect readers – young and old – with the outdoors and the positive impact it can have on well-being. We think it's particularly important that young people get outside and explore the natural world, something we support through our publishing programme.

As well as publishing award-winning new books, we're working to make available many out-of-print classics in both print and digital formats. These are stories that we believe are unique and significant; we want to make sure that they continue to be shared and enjoyed.

www.v-publishing.co.uk

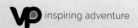

inspiring adventure

Good Run
Guide

The *Good Run Guide* features 40 of the most scenic runs in England and Wales. Ranging in length from 3.4 to 10.7 miles (5.4 to 17.2 kilometres), there are routes for runners of all ability and fitness levels, on a range of surfaces.

Written by experienced runners Louise Piears and Andy Bickerstaff, founders of the Good Run Guide, the UK's leading independent running website, it is an essential glovebox companion for trips away in England and Wales.

Find out more and order direct: **www.v-publishing.co.uk**